Reduce, Reuse, Recycle

Paper

Alexandra Fix

Heinemann Library
Chicago, Illinois

Designed by Steven Mead and Debbie Oatley
Printed in China by South China Printing Company Limited

12 11 10 09 08
10 9 8 7 6 5 4 3 2 1

ISBN 10-digit: 1-4034-9712-5 (hc)   1-4034-9720-6 (pb)

Library of Congress Cataloging-in-Publication Data
Fix, Alexandra, 1950-
  Paper / Alexandra Fix.
    p. cm. -- (Reduce, reuse, recycle)
  Includes bibliographical references and index.
  ISBN 978-1-4034-9712-3 (hc) -- ISBN 978-1-4034-9720-8 (pb)
  1. Waste paper--Recycling--Juvenile literature. 2. Paper products--Juvenile literature. I. Title.
  TD805.F53 2007
  676'.042--dc22
                        2007002784

Acknowledgments
The author and publisher are grateful to the following for permission to reproduce copyright material: Alamy pp. 5 (Julio Ekhart), 6 (Janine Wiedel Photo Library), 8 (Philip Scalia), 12 (Chris Howes/Wild Places Photography), 16 (Directphoto.org), 23 (David R. Frazier Photolibrary), 25 (Neil Cooper); Corbis pp. 4, 7 (Kim Kullish), 9 (Philip Gould), 10 (Frank Lukasseck/Zefa), 11 (Gary Braasch), 13 (Sygma/Langevin Jaques), 15 (Peter Morgan/Reuters), 17 (Jose Luis Pelaez, Inc.), 18 (Paul Almasy), 19 (Jose Luis Pelaez, Inc.), 20 (Karl Weatherly), 21 (Craig Hammell), 22 (Herbert Kehrer/Zefa), 26 (Royalty Free), 27 (Jim Winkley/Ecoscene); Getty Images p. 14 (Photodisc); Harcourt Education p. 29 (Tudor Photography); Science Photo Library p. 24 (Sheila Terry).

Cover photograph reproduced with permission of Corbis/Royalty Free.

Every effort has been made to contact copyright holders of any material reproduced in this book. Any omissions will be rectified in subsequent printings if notice is given to the publisher.

Contents

Some words are shown in bold, **like this**. You can find out what they mean by looking in the glossary.

What Is Paper Waste?

Every day we use paper. We write on notebook paper, read books, and use other paper items. Paper is an important material, but sometimes it is wasted.

Paper is often thrown away.

⟶

4

Paper waste piles up. ↑

Paper waste is paper that is thrown
away. Most paper can be used again
or **recycled**. This wastes less paper.

What Is Made of Paper?

Many items are made of paper. Schools have paper items such as books, notebooks, printer paper, newspapers, and magazines.

Students use many paper items.

Office supply stores sell different types of paper.

Many items from grocery stores come in paper packaging. There are paper towels, napkins, cups, plates, egg cartons, and drink boxes.

Where Does Paper Come From?

Paper is made from trees. To make paper, trees are cut down and the wood is cut into small pieces. These pieces are mixed with water and **chemicals** to make wood **pulp**.

Wood is also used to build houses. ↓

These are large paper rolls at a factory.

Wood pulp is **bleached** white and dried into big sheets of paper. The sheets are made into large rolls of paper. The paper rolls are cut, packaged, and sent to **factories** that make paper items.

Will We Always Have Paper?

Trees are a **renewable resource**. We can grow more trees, but it takes many years for them to grow tall.

In some places, trees are cut down faster than new ones can grow.

These people are planting new trees.

It is important to plant new trees when old trees are cut down. If we reuse or **recycle** paper, fewer trees will have to be cut down.

What Happens When We Waste Paper?

Paper waste is harmful to the **environment**. Paper and cardboard waste take up one-fourth of the space at **landfills**. Landfills are where trash is buried.

Paper buried in landfills gives off a gas that can start fires. ⟶

Chemicals used at paper factories can get into nearby rivers. This can kill fish and plants.

When we waste paper, more paper has to be made. Harmful **chemicals** are released into the air at paper **factories**. Chemicals can also get into the soil.

How Can We Reduce Paper Waste?

Bring your own shopping bag to the grocery store.

We can reduce paper waste by using less paper. Use rags instead of paper towels. Use glass dishes instead of paper plates.

14

Try not to buy things with too much paper packaging. You can also use a cloth bag when you shop instead of getting a new bag each time.

Some toys come in cardboard boxes that can be **recycled**.

How Can We Reuse Paper?

You can reduce paper waste by reusing paper. Write or draw on both sides of a sheet of paper. Use the clean side of scrap paper for printing out documents.

Give away old books to a library or book sale.

Old newspaper can be used for art projects.

Reuse boxes, gift bags, and tissue paper when you give presents. Try wrapping gifts in newspaper or magazines instead of buying new wrapping paper. You can make new gift tags by cutting up old greeting cards.

How Can We Recycle Paper?

When paper is **recycled**, it is broken down and used again to make new paper. Most **communities** have a recycling program for materials such as paper, plastic, glass, and metal.

Many newspapers are printed on recycled paper.

Tie papers of the same type together with string. ↑

To get paper ready for recycling, keep the papers dry. Place papers of the same type together. Separate cardboard, newspaper, and white computer paper.

Where Can We Bring Paper for Recycling?

Recycling trucks pick up items made of paper, plastic, metal, and glass.

In some places, a truck picks up **recycling** items at homes. Then they are brought to a local recycling center.

If your **community** does not have a recycling program, you can bring used paper to a recycling center. From there it gets taken to a **factory**, where it is made into recycled paper.

Paper must be sorted at a recycling center.

How Is Paper Recycled?

At a **recycling** center, paper is separated into newspaper, white paper, and cardboard. It is then pressed into big bundles and taken to a paper **factory**.

These bundles of paper are ready to go to a paper factory.

This wood pulp will become new paper. ↑

Bundles are cut into pieces and mixed with hot water to form **pulp**. The pulp is then cleaned to remove ink, glue, and staples. Recycled pulp is added to new pulp to make paper.

How Do We Use Recycled Paper?

Many things are made of **recycled** paper. Stores sell recycled paper items such as notebook paper, drawing paper, tissues, and paper towels.

Look for the recycle label when you buy paper products.

Recycled paper, cardboard, and glue can be made into paper furniture. ↑

Plasterboard can also be made with recycled paper. Plasterboard is used to make walls in new homes.

How Can You Take Action?

You can help reduce paper waste in your **community**. Ask family and friends to **recycle** paper. Use an old cardboard box to make a recycling box at home.

Put one paper recycling box in your bedroom and another in your kitchen. ↑

You can start a recycling program for other items, too.

Ask your teacher if your class can start reusing and recycling paper. If we all take part, we can reduce paper waste.

Make a Papier Mâché Bowl

Ask an adult to help you with this project.

You will need:

- water
- flour
- permanent marker
- large bowl
- balloon (filled with air)
- empty yogurt container with lid
- strips of newspaper (about two inches wide by five inches long)

1. Mix two cups of flour and two cups of water in a large bowl.
2. Draw a line around the middle of a balloon. Set it in an empty container, knotted side down.
3. Dip the newspaper strips into the mixture. Lay the coated newspaper onto the balloon.
4. Continue to place coated newspaper strips over the surface of the balloon. Overlap each strip

Step 3

Step 7

Step 10

until everything below the line is covered. Then add a second layer of strips.

5. Set the balloon aside to dry overnight.

6. When dry, pop the balloon and remove it from your new bowl.

7. Turn the bowl upside down. Take the lid from the plastic container and tape it onto the bottom. This will give your bowl a flat surface to rest on.

8. Cover the bottom with the coated newspaper strips.

9. Set it aside to dry overnight.

10. You now have a new bowl! Decorate with paints, collage materials, or anything you like.

Glossary

bleach	clean or whiten something using a chemical substance
chemical	basic element that makes up all things
community	group of people who live in one area
environment	natural surroundings for people, animals, and plants
factory	building or buildings where something is made
landfill	large area where trash is dumped, crushed, and covered with soil
pulp	mixture of cut pieces of wood and water
recycle	break down a material and use it again to make a new product. Recycling is the act of breaking down a material and using it again.
renewable resource	something that can be replaced by nature

Find Out More

Books to Read

Galko, Francine. *Earth Friends at School*. Chicago: Heinemann Library, 2004.

Kras, Sara Louise. *Paper*. Mankato, MN: Capstone Press, 2004.

Oxlade, Chris. *How We Use Paper*. Chicago: Raintree, 2005.

Web Sites

The Environmental Protection Agency works to protect the air, water, and land. The organization has a special Web site for students at <u>www.epa.gov/kids</u>.

Earth911 is an organization that gives information about where you can recycle in your community. Their Web site for students is <u>http://www.earth911.org/master.asp?s=kids&a=kids/kids.asp</u>.

Index